When Families Fail

Psychological Disorders Caused by
Parent-Child Relational Problems

THE ENCYCLOPEDIA OF PSYCHOLOGICAL DISORDERS

THE ENCYCLOPEDIA OF PSYCHOLOGICAL DISORDERS

Senior Consulting Editor Carol C. Nadelson, M.D.
Consulting Editor Claire E. Reinburg

When Families Fail,

Psychological Disorders Caused by *C. 1*
Parent-Child Relational Problems

Ann Holmes

CHELSEA HOUSE PUBLISHERS
Philadelphia

The ENCYCLOPEDIA OF PSYCHOLOGICAL DISORDERS provides up-to-date information on the history of, causes and effects of, and treatment and therapies for problems affecting the human mind. The titles in this series are not intended to take the place of the professional advice of a psychiatrist or mental health care professional.

Chelsea House Publishers
Editor in Chief: Stephen Reginald
Managing Editor: James D. Gallagher
Production Manager: Pamela Loos
Art Director: Sara Davis
Director of Photography: Judy L. Hasday
Senior Production Editor: LeeAnne Gelletly

Staff for WHEN FAMILIES FAIL
Prepared by P. M. Gordon Associates, Philadelphia
Picture Researcher: P. M. Gordon Associates
Associate Art Director: Takeshi Takahashi
Cover Designer: Brian Wible

The Chelsea House World Wide Web address is
http://www.chelseahouse.com

First Printing

9 8 7 6 5 4 3 2 1

Library of Congress Cataloging-in-Publication Data

Holmes, Ann.

When Families Fail: psychological disorders caused by parent-child relational problems / by Ann Holmes.
    p.   cm. — (The encyclopedia of psychological disorders)
Includes bibliographical references and index.
ISBN 0-7910-4956-6
1. Problem families—Psychological aspects. 2. Parent and child—Psychological aspects. 3. Families—Mental health. 4. Family—Psychological aspects. I. Title. II. Series.
RC455.4.F3H64   1999
616.89—dc21   99-13291
                                                                       CIP

CONTENTS

PSYCHOLOGICAL DISORDERS AND THEIR EFFECT

CAROL C. NADELSON, M.D.
PRESIDENT AND CHIEF EXECUTIVE OFFICER,
The American Psychiatric Press

There are a wide range of problems that are considered psychological disorders, including mental and emotional disorders, problems related to alcohol and drug abuse, and some diseases that cause both emotional and physical symptoms. Psychological disorders often begin in early childhood, but during adolescence we see a sharp increase in the number of people affected by these disorders. It has been estimated that about 20 percent of the U.S. population will have some form of mental disorder sometime during their lifetime. Some psychological disorders appear following severe stress or trauma. Others appear to occur more often in some families and may have a genetic or inherited component. Still other disorders do not seem to be connected to any cause we can yet identify. There has been a great deal of attention paid to learning about the causes and treatments of these disorders, and exciting new research has taught us a great deal in the past few decades.

The fact that many new and successful treatments are available makes it especially important that we reject old prejudices and outmoded ideas that consider mental disorders to be untreatable. If psychological problems are identified early, it is possible to prevent serious consequences. We should not keep these problems hidden or feel shame that we or a member of our family has a mental disorder. Some people believe that something they said or did caused a mental disorder. Some people think that these disorders are "only in your head" so that you could "snap out of it" if you made the effort. This type of thinking implies that a treatment is a matter of willpower or motivation. It is a terrible burden for someone who is suffering to be blamed for his or her misery, and often people with psychological disorders are not treated compassionately. We hope that the information in this book will teach you about various mental illnesses.

The problems covered in the volumes in the ENCYCLOPEDIA OF PSYCHOLOGICAL DISORDERS were selected because they are of particular importance to young adults, because they affect them directly or because they affect family and friends. There are individual volumes on reading disorders, attention deficit and disruptive behavior disorders, and dementia—all of these are related to our abilities to learn and integrate information from the world around us. There are books on drug abuse that provide useful information about the effects of these drugs and treatments that are available for those individuals who have drug problems. Some of the books concentrate on one of the most common mental disorders, depression. Others deal with eating disorders, which are dangerous illnesses that affect a large number of young adults, especially women.

Most of the public attention paid to these disorders arises from a particular incident involving a celebrity that awakens us to our own vulnerability to psychological problems. These incidents of celebrities or public figures revealing their own psychological problems can also enable us to think about what we can do to prevent and treat these types of problems.

DYSFUNCTIONAL FAMILIES: AN OVERVIEW

In recent years, there has been a great deal of discussion about "dysfunctional" families, but what exactly is a dysfunctional family? What, for that matter, is a functional family? And when does a family cross the line from experiencing the normal conflicts that occur in all relationships to being out of control and destructive?

Many people are raised in loving and supportive families, but the perfect family doesn't exist. At times, all family members fight, bicker, and have misunderstandings. Even the best parents have moments when they are unable to provide their children with the emotional support that is needed. Everyone in a family makes mistakes, and these mistakes can bring a great deal of pain to other family members.

Nevertheless, in functional families—families that work—all members are secure in the knowledge that they are loved and that the other family members will always be there for them. In these families, members are cheered on when they do well and encouraged when they encounter problems.

Unfortunately, many families don't function this well. For a variety of reasons, children are expected to carry adult responsibilities, and one or both parents are allowed to be childishly irresponsible. This volume of the ENCYCLOPEDIA OF PSYCHOLOGICAL DISORDERS explores the history of such family problems, why they arise, what happens to children who grow up in a dysfunctional environment, and the kinds of therapy that are available.

A dysfunctional family fails to provide its children with a nurturing environment, and the effects can be seen for decades—even generations—afterward.

1

WHAT IS A DYSFUNCTIONAL FAMILY?

In a recent case in Pittsburgh, reported in the *Pittsburgh Post-Gazette*, a young mother in her late teens left her 11-month-old son locked in their home by himself while she attended a job training program. The child was left on a mattress near a space heater with faulty wiring. The mattress ignited, and the child died in the resulting fire.

Another case, described by Susan Forward in her book *Toxic Parents*, involves a young man named Glenn, who grew up with a father who was an alcoholic. Drinking controlled their family. Every night after his father had passed out from drinking, Glenn and his mother and sisters would put the man to bed. Glenn's job was to remove his father's shoes and socks. For a long time, he thought this was a normal part of any family's life. His father would often become violent. When Glenn's father attacked his mother, she would run to Glenn and ask him what she should do. Even as a young boy, Glenn thought it was his job to take care of his mother and protect her from his father.

In yet another family, discussed in the book *Facing Codependence*, four-year-old Mary, like most four-year-olds, wasn't yet fully coordinated. Because of this, she sometimes spilled her milk. Instead of taking such accidents in stride, her mother would say, "Shame on you for spilling the milk. You're a bad little girl. Good girls don't spill their milk. Don't ever do that again."

While on the surface these examples are quite different, they share a common theme. In each situation, parents expected their children to act in ways they were not equipped to do, and the parents did not provide their children with a nurturing environment. Simply put, the family didn't function correctly. It was dysfunctional.

"Functional" means able to operate or work, and a *functional family* is one that works. A *dysfunctional family* is one that doesn't work, doesn't do its job. But what is a family in modern terms, and what is its job?

WHAT IS A FAMILY?

Although everyone has a vision, based on his or her own experience, of what a family is or isn't, a *family* can be defined as a group of people related by marriage, biology, or adoption, or who cooperatively share a residence on a long-term basis. Since the beginning of human history, families in every culture have had the primary responsibility for having children and teaching them how to function in life.

The word "family" is used broadly and loosely. It can refer to a married couple and their children; a single parent and his or her children; a group that shares a common ancestry; or any small, close-knit group that feels a sense of belonging. A group of close friends may refer to themselves as a family.

A *nuclear family* is made up of a husband, a wife, and their children, living in an independent or separate household. In some cultures, polygyny (a husband with more than one wife) or polyandry (a wife with more than one husband) is considered a sign of social status.

A *consanguineal family* is made up of a single parent and his or her children. A *blended family* consists of a parent, stepparent, and children and stepchildren. *Complex families* are based either on generational ties (including grandparents or great-grandparents) or lateral ties (including aunts, uncles, and cousins). Other family types include less formal arrangements, such as couples who live together without being married.

ROLE OF THE FAMILY

In the past, families were relatively elastic units that served a wide range of social functions. Families were the basic economic unit of society, supporting themselves through hunting and farming. They also educated the young and cared for the sick and elderly. Families were flexible enough to take in extended relatives or friends as well.

During the 19th and 20th centuries, especially in Western nations, the family lost or changed many of its traditional economic, educational, and social roles, and its boundaries became increasingly rigid. Today, relatively few Western families take in relatives or friends, and government and private businesses or social organizations have assumed many of the family's traditional functions.

For example, consider a mother with two young children who is deserted by her husband. In the past, the mother and her children would most likely have been cared for by her own parents or by other family members. Now, however, this family will probably seek help through a

The traditional nuclear family, like this mother and father with their two biological children, remains common in the United States, but many families are now different in structure.

family shelter and receive food, clothing, and child-care services from government or private agencies.

Despite these changes, the family remains modern society's most important unit for raising children and providing emotional support for its members. The main functions of a family are having children; caring for those children; teaching the children about society and how they will find a place in it; and establishing sexual controls. These family functions are the same in any society. Since they are the core functions of social life, the family is the basic instrument through which all other activities operate, whether political, religious, or economic.

All of these activities can be carried on or supported by other institutions. For example, a child can be given a social rank or class based on talent or intelligence, rather than on membership in a particular family. And governmental agencies or relatives other than the parents can care for and train children. Schools, churches, and other agencies can instill sexual values.

However, it is by combining these important functions that the family is most effective. By confining legitimate reproduction to the family, societies fix responsibility for the physical care and social training of children on the parents. Parents therefore become responsible for developing their children's ability to deal with others. Mothers and fathers pass along the customs of their own background, so their children generally attain the same social status as the parents. The functions of care and training are best combined because they have a direct impact on socialization—how the child adapts to being with other people.

CHANGES IN FAMILY STRUCTURE

Many Americans have a concept of "family" that no longer matches reality. In the 1950s, American television programs showed idealized families, images that became a guideline for what people thought their own families should be. Shows like *Ozzie and Harriet* and *Leave It to Beaver* portrayed happy, comfortable, middle-class families in which the father went off each morning to a well-paying white-collar job, Mom stayed home to cook and clean (in a dress and high-heeled shoes), and the children, even if mischievous, were respectful and obedient. Besides minimizing the problems of family life, these shows helped foster an image of family structure that has become increasingly inaccurate.

As recently as 1960, 70 percent of all U.S. households did consist of a breadwinner father, a homemaker mother, and two or more children, similar to the families in those early television shows. By 1996, however, this was the case in only about 20 percent of American households. Why did such a dramatic change occur?

One reason is that, in the United States as well as other Western countries, mothers have entered the paid workforce in record numbers. As recently as 1940, less than 12 percent of white married women in the United States were in the work force; by 1990 the figure reached nearly 60 percent, and it has continued to rise. In 1998 the Kids Count project estimated that 70 percent of all U.S. women with preschool children would be working in 2000.

Additionally, the U.S. divorce rate more than doubled between 1965 and 1979. Although the rate began to decline slightly in the 1990s, it is still quite high. Each year, for every 1,000 married women in the United

The TV show Leave It to Beaver, *popular in the 1950s, portrayed a happy family with a working father, a stay-at-home mother, and their two biological children. Many Americans still consider such a family ideal, but the typical structure of American families has changed dramatically since then.*

A single mother gets ready for work while her 13-year-old daughter makes a lunch to take to school. The number of such American families—a single woman living with her children—has more than tripled since the late 1950s.

States, there will be about 20 divorces. The net result is that approximately 10 percent of the U.S. adult population is currently divorced.

The rising divorce rate, in turn, has contributed to a sharp increase in the number of single-parent households. The number of households consisting of a single mother and her children more than tripled from the late 1950s to the late 1990s. Also adding to the increase in female-headed homes was a sharp rise in the number of out-of-wedlock births. Five percent of births in 1965 were to unmarried mothers; by 1996, nearly 33 percent were born to an unmarried mother. Meanwhile, with more mothers working outside the home, an increasing number of young children were being cared for during the day by adults other than a parent.

The rate of cohabitation (living together) outside of marriage has increased, but rather than replacing marriage, living together usually appears to be a temporary stage prior to marriage or remarriage. Although growing numbers of American men and women have postponed marriage into their late twenties or early thirties, approximately 19 out of 20 Americans marry before they reach middle age.

Nevertheless, the individual nuclear family is highly fragile. In a society noted for impersonal, competitive relations, it is the one unit that is supposed to support the individual with love and stable affection. While the emotional demands made upon the family are great, the ideal of romantic love lends an unrealistic note to the marriage bond. If romantic happiness fades, many couples feel there is no point in staying married. What is more, family, friends, and even religious groups may no longer put great pressure on couples to stay together. Many people no longer consider divorce to be shocking or undesirable.

Despite these changes in the family structure, family relationships generally remain strong in the United States. It is important to recognize, though, that the modern family has undergone many changes and faces great potential for internal tension and external stress. Given these circumstances, it is easy to see why some families become dysfunctional.

WHEN THE FAMILY BREAKS DOWN

We've taken a look at the family and what it is supposed to do, and we have some understanding of the stresses that families face. When a family starts to fail in its mission to provide a flexible, supportive environment for its members, it becomes dysfunctional. It doesn't work. In

FAMILY CHANGES AROUND THE WORLD

Throughout the world, families have changed significantly since the beginning of the 20th century. In the developing world, urbanization (the growth of cities), economic modernization (including the spread of industry and the growth of a cash economy), contact with Western societies, and improvements in the status of women have produced broad changes in family patterns in the past hundred years. These changes include the following:

- A drop in death and birth rates
- A decline in polygamy and arranged marriages (in which parents choose the spouses for their children)
- Decreasing numbers of extended families
- Increasing numbers of nuclear-family households

In addition, divorce has become available in areas where it once was forbidden by religion or cultural traditions.

In industrial nations, too, new family patterns have emerged. One of the more striking is the appearance of love as a basis for marriage. Although romantic love has been criticized as a poor basis for stable family life, it does draw couples into marriage in a society where marriages are not arranged. Romantic love also holds many couples together long enough to build a strong relationship that leads to a continuing marriage.

short, a dysfunctional family does not provide a healthy environment in which its members can grow.

Although modern families face many pressures, dysfunctional families are nothing new, and there are many examples that go back to the earliest recorded times. In fact, the Bible's "first family," Adam and Eve, is a classic example. Rather than offering each other support, Adam and Eve both gave in to temptation to eat a forbidden piece of fruit, then blamed each other when they were found out. After being banished from the Garden of Eden, they had two sons, Abel and Cain. In a fit of jealousy, Cain killed his brother Abel. The Old Testament is as full of tales of incest, deception, jealousy, and murder as any popular daytime television drama.

Beyond leading to an unhealthy or unhappy way of life, dysfunctional families may actually cause psychological or physical harm to their members.

DYSFUNCTIONAL FAMILY PATTERNS

Because a major purpose of a family is to raise children, children are often the focus of family life. Ideally, children grow up in families that help them feel worthwhile and valuable. They learn that their feelings and needs are important and can be expressed. Children growing up in such supportive environments are likely to form healthy, open relationships as adults.

However, families may fail to provide for their children's emotional and physical needs. In addition, families may not permit children to express their feelings and needs, or parents may play down children's serious fears or concerns. The following patterns occur frequently in dysfunctional families:

- One or both parents have addictions or compulsions (e.g., drugs, alcohol, promiscuity, gambling, overworking, over-dedication to a religion or cause, and/or overeating) that impact other family members.

- One or both parents use threats of or actual physical violence as the primary means of control. Children may be forced to witness violence, required to participate in punishing siblings, or made to live in fear of explosive verbal outbursts.

- One or both parents exploit the children and treat them as possessions whose primary purpose is to respond to the physical and/or emotional needs of adults (such as protecting a parent who is abused or cheering up one who is depressed).

- One or both parents are unable to provide, or threaten to withdraw, financial or basic physical care for their children. Similarly, one or both parents fail to provide their children with adequate emotional support.

- One or both parents exert strong authoritarian control over the children. Often these families rigidly adhere to a particular belief system (religious, political, financial, or personal). Children are expected to obey without asking questions, and there is no flexibility within the family.

Every family has moments when it isn't functioning well. But there is a great deal of variety both in how often dysfunctional behavior occurs in families and in the kinds and severity of the dysfunction. When patterns such as the above are the rule and not the exception, however, family members are likely to be experiencing abuse or neglect.

CHILDREN IN DYSFUNCTIONAL FAMILIES

In dysfunctional families, children may be forced to take sides in conflicts between the parents, or may be used as "go-betweens" who report back to the other parent. Rather than dealing with their problems as adults, the parents put the weight of their conflict on their children. As families break apart, children may even be forced to choose which parent they want to continue living with and may be restricted from full and direct communication or contact with other family members.

Children in dysfunctional families may experience "reality shifting" between what is said and what is true. For example, they may witness their father hit or otherwise abuse their mother, only to have one—or both—parents later deny that the abuse ever occurred.

Children may be ignored, discounted, or criticized for their feelings and thoughts, which can damage their self-esteem and self-confidence. They may feel that their needs and ideas are not important or perhaps should not be taken seriously by others. As a result, they may form negative self-images and unsatisfying relationships as adults.

Dysfunctional parents may be either distant and uninvolved with their children or, at the opposite end, be inappropriately intrusive, involved, and overly protective.

Children in dysfunctional families may be too structured, with unrealistic demands placed on their time, choice of friends, achievements, or behavior. In some overly demanding families, children may be taken from soccer practice to swimming, to gymnastics, to music lessons, to play rehearsal without any time to be on their own. This overload of activities is scheduled not to support the special interests of the children but rather to push the children into fulfilling the unrealistic expectations of the parents. At the other extreme, the children may receive no guidelines or structure at all. They are expected to fend for themselves

WHERE TO GET HELP FOR ABUSE

In some dysfunctional families, physical violence takes place. Children may be victims, witnesses, or participants. Thankfully, resources exist to protect family members from being abused. If you or someone you know is in immediate physical danger, call 911 or your local police. If there is physical or sexual abuse involved, tell a teacher, guidance counselor, family doctor, member of the clergy, or other trusted adult.

Toll-free hotlines are available 24 hours a day. One such national hotline is the National Domestic Violence Hotline at 1-800-799-7233, which offers confidential and immediate help in English or Spanish and has interpreters available to translate an additional 139 languages. This hotline links callers to help in their local area. It has a nationwide database that includes detailed information on domestic violence and other emergency shelters, as well as legal advocacy and assistance programs and social service programs.

and to figure out what proper behavior and relationships are. In both situations, children are being forced to accept adult responsibilities for which they are ill-equipped.

Although in any family it is difficult not to compare children, some parents constantly compare their children's abilities. The problem with comparisons is that there is always a negative. For every "smart one," there is necessarily a "stupid one." For every "pretty one," there must be an "ugly one." Even if parents don't intend to create these negatives, the children still experience either rejection or unhealthy preferential treatment because of the comparisons.

In dysfunctional families, children may be allowed or encouraged to use drugs or alcohol. In an interview with *TV Guide*, Mackenzie Phillips, an actress and the daughter of John Phillips of the 1960s pop group the Mamas and the Papas, tells about battling a lifelong drug and alcohol addiction that began when she started rolling joints for her father at age 10.

In some dysfunctional families, children are frequently criticized or blamed, even for things that aren't their fault.

Physical punishment or abuse in dysfunctional families can be intense. Children may be locked out of the house, slapped, hit, scratched, punched, or kicked for what many families would consider minor violations. Author Christina Crawford, one of the adopted children of film star Joan Crawford, led a seemingly ideal, privileged life in Hollywood in the 1940s and 1950s. As an adult, though, she wrote a chilling memoir of her childhood, *Mommie Dearest*, that told of being locked in the closet and beaten with hangers.

Abuse and neglect inhibit the development of children's trust in the world, in others, and in themselves. Later, as adults, they may find it difficult to trust the behavior and words of others, their own judgments and actions, or their own sense of self-worth. Not surprisingly, they may experience problems in their work, their relationships, and their very identities.

As adults, abused and neglected family members often attempt to interpret their family's behavior as "normal." But the more they try to make the situation seem normal ("I wasn't beaten, just spanked"), the more likely they will misinterpret themselves and develop negative self-concepts ("If I hadn't been bad, I wouldn't have been spanked").

Many people who grow up in dysfunctional families hope that once they leave home, they will put their family and childhood problems behind them. Unfortunately, most of them discover that they experience similar problems, as well as similar feelings and relationship patterns, long after they leave home.

In past centuries, just as today, families in crisis were often counseled by a clergyman or relative.

2

THE FAMILY SYSTEM

Although dysfunctional families have existed throughout history, the formal study of these families and the commitment to developing ways of helping them is a fairly recent development.

One of the first professionals to describe symptoms that mark some dysfunctional family members was Emil Kraepelin, who in 1913 wrote of the "irresoluteness of will" that marked such dependent patients. Other professionals, including Karl Abraham in the 1920s, Erich Fromm in the 1940s, and Karen Horney in the 1950s, described similar symptoms among their patients, but little follow-up was done.

Researchers focused mainly on one family relationship—the mother-child relationship during early childhood. They assumed that deficiencies in the mother's personality and mothering style were responsible for any disturbance in the child. Most psychiatrists focused on individuals and their specific problems rather than on how groups of people functioned, or failed to function, together. Family members (if they were considered at all) were generally viewed as separate from the issues involved in the individual treatment of the patient.

This attitude changed in the 1950s and 1960s. As more professionals worked to solve the problems of drug and alcohol dependency as well as major psychiatric disorders such as schizophrenia, researchers began to make observations about the families from which their patients came. These observations led to a breakthrough in thinking about how the family affects the problems individuals face, as well as how an individual's problems affect his or her family.

THE PATIENT-FAMILY RELATIONSHIP

The therapists noticed two types of behaviors among the family members of their chemically dependent patients. In the first type, family members worked very hard to be "perfect" in everything they did for the patient in

Psychiatry in the early 20th century often attributed childhood disturbances to problems with the mother's personality or her style of parenting. It was not until the 1950s and 1960s that professionals began to see the entire family as a system.

hopes that their "perfect" behavior would help the patient break free from his or her chemical dependency. When they didn't see the hoped-for results, these family members became angry. But they couldn't express their anger directly at the family member with the chemical dependency. Instead they would use indirect methods such as sarcasm, forgetfulness, hostile jokes, and other passive-aggressive behaviors. They would also overreact to normal events and become extremely angry with people who hadn't done anything to deserve such a reaction.

In the second type of behavior, family members minimized their feelings, sometimes to the point of being numb. No matter what happened, they rarely felt fear, pain, anger, shame, joy, pleasure, contentment—it was as if they were sleepwalking through life.

When therapists began these studies, they thought that the unhealthy behavior of their patients' family members was the result of the stress of living with someone who was chemically dependent. But then the therapists noticed something. When, for example, an alcoholic would stop drinking, the rest of the family often continued behaving in unhealthy ways. These family members would sometimes even work to sabotage the progress that the patient had made, as if they needed the patient to remain sick and dependent on them.

Further study revealed that many of the families' unhealthy behavior patterns had existed before the patients became alcoholics or drug addicts. Tracing the possible sources for these patterns, therapists found that, in many cases, one or more of the family members had themselves been abused during childhood or had grown up with a parent or parents who were alcoholics or drug addicts.

An alcoholic mother struggles to help her child with an ordinary task. Studies of alcoholics have shown that their personal behavior is connected in complex ways to unhealthy patterns in the family.

From this research, the field of family therapy was born. During the past three decades, family therapists have been developing a number of approaches to help people break the unhealthy patterns of behavior that so often develop in dysfunctional families, and celebrities such as talk-show host Oprah Winfrey have done much to popularize the therapists' findings.

TREATING THE FAMILY

Family therapy has become one of the major approaches to understanding individual and family problems. It attempts to solve individual problems by studying how the patient's family functions. A key to the approach is the consideration of the entire family as a *system*, that is, a group of interacting and interrelated elements.

Seen as a system, the family as a whole is greater than the sum of its parts; it cannot be described simply by summing up characteristics of individual members. To understand a family, one must consider its organization and the way its members act toward one another.

Family-systems therapists see the family as an ever-changing unit that functions in relation to its larger environment. The family is made of subsystems: for instance, the interactions among the children form one subsystem, and the parents as a couple form another subsystem. The family also interacts with other systems, such as those involving work and school.

The assumption in the family-systems approach is that an individual's behavior is greatly influenced by the way other family members act. Therefore, the most effective way to change the person is to change the system in which he or she is living. Therapy may involve sessions with the entire family, individual sessions with the patient or other family members, or a combination of different types of sessions.

Because problems are viewed in the context of the family, what is normal or abnormal is defined to fit the individual and family situation. For instance, in a family in which members always function independently, with each person fending for himself or herself, a crisis requiring close teamwork might trigger dysfunction because the family's style conflicts with the immediate demands.

The family systems approach assumes that most families have strengths and weaknesses, and that dysfunction can emerge in certain situations or at different stages of family or individual life. It's interesting, too, that the same situation may cause one family to experience dys-

The family systems approach: A behavioral health therapist (far left) addresses her efforts not just to the 11-year-old girl who has behavior problems, but to the other members of the girl's family as well.

function while a second family may rally and pull together to deal with the problem.

BREAKING UNHEALTHY PATTERNS

Because family members are in close contact with each other, a change in any one member affects the group as a whole, which in turn affects the individual. Every action causes a reaction. So to help solve a problem, it's important to know what causes family relations to improve, worsen, or remain the same.

For instance, a therapist asks a man who is depressed what his wife does when he acts depressed. He answers, "She becomes critical." The therapist then asks how the man responds to his wife's criticism. "I get angry at her and more despondent," the man replies. This reveals a

IS SOMEONE YOU KNOW BEING ABUSED?

F amily therapists devise careful treatment plans on the basis of the entire family organization, and they generally try not to be judgmental or to have fixed notions of what is "normal." When the family pattern involves obvious abuse, however, immediate action is necessary. If you think someone you know is being abused, either physically or emotionally, look for the following indicators:

- Does he or she appear anxious, depressed, withdrawn, and reluctant to talk?
- Do parents or other family members criticize this person in front of you, making remarks that make you feel uncomfortable?
- Do you see or hear about repeated bruises, broken bones, or other injuries that reportedly result from "accidents"?
- Does a family member try to control this person's every move, making him or her account for each minute spent away from home?
- Is this person often late or absent from school, has this person quit school altogether, or does this person regularly leave social functions early because a family member is waiting?

If you answered yes to any of these questions, talk to a trusted adult or a domestic violence hotline (such as the National Domestic Violence Hotline: 1-800-799-7233) about the situation.

Source: National Domestic Violence Hotline, http://www.ndvh.org/.

behavioral pattern within the family that adds to the man's basic problem of depression.

Planning for therapy takes these kinds of family patterns into consideration and aims to break the patterns in order to help solve the problem. However, not everyone in an unhealthy family pattern is equally to blame or equally at risk. When a child is being abused, the abuser must be held responsible for his or her actions, regardless of what the child might be doing to trigger a reaction. No behavior on the part of the child justifies abuse. Even if a child has been whining or misbehaving, a parent or caregiver has choices about how to respond. Abuse is never an appropriate response.

AVOIDING LABELS

Researchers have found no one-to-one connection between an individual's problems and a particular pattern of family dysfunction. It would be wrong to label a family based on the problem that one of its members faces.

For example, since no single pattern has been found to distinguish all families with a child who is schizophrenic, a label such as "schizophrenic family" wrongly implies that the parents are to blame for the child's illness. Such a label fails to recognize the diversity of family styles and levels of functioning that are present in families facing conditions like schizophrenia.

The family-systems approach recognizes that psychiatric problems may be primarily based on a physical condition, as in schizophrenia, or they may be a reaction to social or economic pressures. Family dysfunction may be caused by many factors: the strain of coping with a family member's chronic illness; an overload of external stress, such as job loss and economic strain; or a crisis, such as traumatic loss or death in the family. All influences must be considered carefully.

This crying child is receiving the emotional support he needs from his mother. In dysfunctional families, by contrast, the children often get either too little support or too much.

3

HOW CHILDREN ARE AFFECTED

Children who grow up in dysfunctional families work hard just to survive. Usually they don't realize that their family shouldn't act the way it does until either there is some outside intervention or they become older and begin to compare the way their family functions with the way they see other families functioning. Because they think their family represents the way families are supposed to be, they try very hard to make the family system work.

■   ■   ■

Les's mother spent most of her time in her bathrobe, and she didn't talk much. Rather than taking care of Les and his younger brothers, she spent hours watching TV. Les's father was a traveling salesman, and when he was in town, he often worked 16-hour days. As Susan Forward describes in her book *Toxic Parents*, Les's father often told him, "Don't forget to do all your homework, and be sure to take care of your mother. Make sure she has enough to eat. Keep the other kids quiet . . . and see if you can do something to get a smile out of her."

Les didn't know that he shouldn't be expected to take care of his younger brothers and his mother. So, beginning when he was eight years old, he made sure his brothers had meals to eat, packed their school lunches, got them to the bus stop on time, went to school, and then came home, cooked dinner, and cleaned the house. He rarely was able to go outside and play with friends. When Forward told Les that she ached for how lonely that little boy must have been, he said, "I had too much to do to feel sorry for myself."

No matter how hard Les worked to make his mother smile, he never succeeded. But no one told him that it wasn't his job to make his mother happy. So he continued to try to succeed and continued to fail. "I was so sure there was something that I could do and everything would be okay again . . . *she'd* be okay again," Les said. "But no matter what I did, nothing changed. It still hasn't. I really feel rotten about that."

CHILDREN'S SYMPTOMS

Les isn't alone. In *Facing Codependence*, Pia Mellody and her coauthors identify five symptoms that children raised in dysfunctional families often develop. These children have difficulty (both as children and as adults) in the following areas:

- Experiencing appropriate levels of self-esteem

- Setting functional boundaries

- Owning and expressing their own reality

- Taking care of their adult needs and wants

- Experiencing and expressing their reality moderately

The first symptom, "experiencing appropriate levels of self-esteem," refers to the tendency to either think too much or too little of oneself. Children who are treated by their family as if they can do no wrong often feel superior to other people. Their parents don't confront or correct them when they make mistakes, and these children are not taught to be responsible for their actions.

On the other hand, children who are constantly given the message that they can't do anything right or that they are not living up to their parents' expectations (like Les) begin to think everyone else is better than they are. Their self-esteem is low or nonexistent.

The second symptom in Mellody's list refers to *boundaries*, which are invisible fences we erect both to keep people from coming into our space and abusing us and to keep us from going into other people's space and abusing them. Young children don't have these boundaries and need to be both protected by their parents and taught appropriate behavior toward others.

Usually, in dysfunctional families, children either are not given enough protection or are overprotected. In both cases they don't learn how to set proper boundaries for themselves. Children who aren't taught how to set boundaries are easily abused and often become abusers. Sometimes, in reaction to the overly vulnerable positions they find themselves in, they develop walls of anger or fear. They shut out people they love because they are afraid of being abused.

The third symptom on the list concerns children's understanding of reality. Children raised in dysfunctional families often doubt their perceptions of reality. They hear or see their parents fighting but then are told that no fight took place. They get good grades in school but are told they are stupid. In one case, an 11-year-old girl was constantly told by her father that she smelled bad even though she showered three times a day, wore perfume, and applied deodorant liberally. Children from dysfunctional families often have doubts about their reality. They are not sure how they look and what their body senses, what they think and whether they can share that information with others, how they feel, and what they should or should not do. In some cases, they are over-

Reality often appears in extremes for children from dysfunctional families. Some, like this boy, may feel they are utterly alone, without a friend in the world.

whelmed by their feelings or have a hard time taking responsibility for their behavior and its effect on other people.

The fourth symptom often found in people who grow up in dysfunctional families is difficulty in acknowledging and meeting their own needs and wants. Like Les, many children in dysfunctional families are told that they alone must take care of a parent and/or their siblings. When they become adults, they refuse to ask other people for help in getting their own needs met because they never received such help when they were growing up. And they never learn that rest and relaxation are legitimate needs for everyone—including themselves.

Some children in dysfunctional families never learn the difference between needs and wants. Parents give their children every material thing they could ever want but never supply the physical and emotional nurturing they need. When these children become adults, they are often totally unaware of their real needs. Instead they spend their time and money acquiring as many things as they can get their hands on. But they ignore their real needs for emotional intimacy and supportive relationships.

The last symptom Mellody identifies in children from dysfunctional families is difficulty experiencing and expressing reality in a moderate way. These children tend to live life at extremes. They are exhilaratingly happy or absolutely miserable. They are either incredibly involved or extremely detached. A middle ground doesn't exist for them.

This lack of a middle ground often expresses itself in four areas: (1) the body, (2) thinking, (3) feelings, and (4) behavior. Children from dysfunctional families tend to dress either with the goal of hiding their bodies—wearing very bland clothing or baggy clothing that completely covers their bodies—or so wildly that everyone stares at them. The children may also be compulsively neat or sloppy about their personal grooming. They tend to think in terms of black and white, right or wrong, good and bad. Their feelings are either numb or explosively agonizing. And their behavior tends to fall at one extreme or another—they don't trust anyone or they trust everyone; they don't let anyone touch them at all or they let everyone touch them.

In addition to causing these five symptoms, dysfunctional family relations can aggravate serious psychological disorders. These include a wide range of mood and personality disorders that can be seen in young children or in adults who had disruptive family lives. The rest of this chapter explores some of the links between psychological disorders and family dysfunction.

Note, however, that not everyone who suffers from psychological disorders comes from a dysfunctional family. Nor, in most cases, can we be sure whether the family dysfunction brought on the individual's psychological problems or vice versa. What does seem clear, from the family-systems approach, is that everyone in the family affects everyone else. With that in mind, let's look at some of the psychological disorders often found in dysfunctional families.

MOOD DISORDERS

A key mood disorder found in some dysfunctional families is *depression*, in which people lose interest or pleasure in nearly all activities. They may experience a change in appetite or weight; problems sleeping; decreased energy; feelings of worthlessness or guilt; difficulty thinking, concentrating, or making decisions; or recurrent thoughts of death or suicide.

In a period of major depression, according to the fourth edition of the *Diagnostic and Statistical Manual of Mental Disorders (DSM-IV)*, people may feel sad, hopeless, discouraged, or "down in the dumps." In some cases, they may at first deny feeling these symptoms. Some people may complain of feeling "blah," having no feelings, or feeling anxious, or they may have bodily aches and pains rather than feelings of sadness.

People suffering from depression may be persistently angry and show a tendency to respond to events with angry outbursts or by blaming others. They may experience an exaggerated sense of frustration over minor matters. Depressed children and adolescents may develop an irritable or cranky mood rather than a sad or dejected mood.

Almost always, depressed people lose interest or pleasure in things, at least to some degree. They may report feeling less interested in hobbies, "not caring anymore," or not feeling any enjoyment in activities that were once fun. Family members often notice that the depressed person withdraws from or neglects activities that usually are enjoyed, such as a child who used to look forward to soccer but now finds excuses not to practice.

Typically, depressed people experience a loss of appetite, and many feel that they have to force themselves to eat. Adults may lose significant amounts of weight, and children may fail to make expected weight gains.

A mood disorder in one family member can affect the entire family.

Depression is associated with sleep disturbances, most commonly insomnia. Individuals typically have middle insomnia (waking up during the night and having difficulty returning to sleep) or terminal insomnia (waking too early and being unable to return to sleep). Initial insomnia (difficulty falling asleep) may also occur. Less frequently, individuals may oversleep (hypersomnia) by either sleeping longer at night or spending more time sleeping during the day.

Depressed people may be agitated—unable to sit still, constantly pacing, wringing their hands, or making other repetitive movements. Others may exhibit depression with opposite symptoms: their speech may slow down, and their thought processes and body movements may be slower than usual. Decreased energy, tiredness, and fatigue are common. Depressed people often report long periods of fatigue when they haven't been physically active. Even the smallest tasks seem to require a huge effort, and often tasks aren't accomplished as efficiently as usual. For example, sometimes depressed people complain that taking a shower, brushing their teeth, and getting dressed in the morning are exhausting activities that take twice as long as usual.

The sense of worthlessness or guilt associated with depression may include unrealistically negative evaluations of one's worth or guilty preoccupations with minor failings from the past. These individuals often misinterpret neutral or trivial day-to-day events as evidence of personal defects and have an exaggerated sense of responsibility for events beyond their control. For example, a real estate agent may become preoccupied with failing to make sales even when the local real estate market has collapsed and other realtors are equally unable to make sales.

Many depressed individuals report having difficulty thinking, concentrating, or making decisions. They may appear easily distracted or complain of memory difficulties. People in demanding jobs are often unable to function adequately even when they have mild concentration problems. A computer programmer, for instance, may discover she can no longer perform complicated but previously manageable tasks. In children, a drop in grades may reflect poor concentration.

Depressed children sometimes experience separation anxiety—the fear of being away from a parent. Marital problems (such as divorce), occupational problems (such as loss of one's job), academic problems (such as truancy or failing grades), and alcohol or other substance abuse may also accompany depression.

In addition to depressed episodes, people who live in dysfunctional families may experience violent upswings in mood. *Manic* episodes are distinct periods during which people have abnormally elevated, expansive, euphoric, or irritable moods that last at least one week. During a manic episode they may be easily distracted and need less sleep. If this elevated mood is combined with the symptoms of depression every day

This mother's personality disorder affects the behavior patterns of her husband and her son, and they in turn will affect the course of her disorder.

for at least a week, the patient is said to be undergoing a "mixed" episode.

PERSONALITY DISORDERS

The stress of a dysfunctional family life is also a risk factor for specific personality disorders. *Personality disorders* are patterns of inner experience and behavior that are extremely different from the expectations of the person's culture, are pervasive and inflexible, begin in adolescence or early adulthood, become stable over time, and lead to distress or impairment.

Major personality disorders include the following patterns:

- *Schizoid personality disorder:* detachment from social relationships and a limited range of emotional expression

- *Schizotypal personality disorder:* acute discomfort in close relationships, distortions in perceptions, and eccentricities of behavior

- *Antisocial personality disorder:* disregard for and violation of the rights of others

- *Borderline personality disorder:* instability in interpersonal relationships and self-image that is marked by impulsive behavior

- *Histrionic personality disorder:* a pattern of excessive emotionality and attention seeking

- *Avoidant personality disorder:* social inhibition, feelings of inadequacy, and hypersensitivity to negative evaluation

- *Dependent personality disorder:* submissive and clinging behavior related to an excessive need to be taken care of

- *Obsessive-compulsive personality disorder:* preoccupation with orderliness, perfectionism, and control

Again, it is important to realize that dysfunctional families do not necessarily *cause* such disorders, nor does the family have to be dysfunctional for the disorder to appear. Still, family dysfunction seems to heighten the risk that individuals will develop a personality disorder— and, conversely, the presence of such a disorder seems to increase the chances of family dysfunction.

OTHER DISORDERS

A dysfunctional family may also influence the severity of other childhood disorders, including these:

- *Learning disorders:* academic functioning that is much lower than expected given the person's age, intelligence, and education

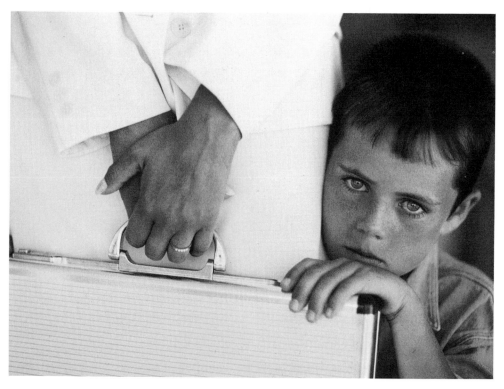

A child with separation anxiety disorder feels excessive apprehension about being separated from parents or other loved ones.

- *Communication disorders*: difficulties in speech or language, such as stuttering

- *Attention-deficit disorders*: prominent inattention and/or hyperactivity-impulsivity

- *Disruptive behavior disorders*: a pattern of behavior that ignores the basic rights of others or that is negative, hostile, and defiant

- *Feeding and eating disorders* of infancy or early childhood: persistent disturbances in feeding and eating

- *Tic disorders*: vocal and/or motor tics

A wide variety of other disorders can also relate to dysfunctional family life. *Separation anxiety disorder* is characterized by excessive anxiety about separation from home or from those to whom the child is attached. *Selective mutism* is a consistent failure to speak in specific social situations despite the ability to speak in other situations. *Reactive attachment disorder* of infancy or early childhood is characterized by markedly disturbed and developmentally inappropriate social action in most situations. *Stereotypic movement disorder* is characterized by repetitive, seemingly driven, and nonfunctional motor behavior that markedly interferes with normal activities and at times may result in bodily injury.

Obviously, the stresses of dysfunctional family life have a major impact on the psychological well-being of all family members, whether child or adult, and the effects may last well beyond childhood.

Poverty and substandard housing are obvious problems for this aboriginal family in northern Australia. But all families face challenges of some sort—physical or emotional, dramatic or subtle. The way a family organizes itself to meet its challenges is a key to successful family functioning.

4

HOW FAMILIES BREAK DOWN

From studying dysfunctional families as a whole and individuals who make up these families, psychiatrists have identified four significant components in a family that can break down: organizational patterns, communication and problem solving, life-cycle development, and belief systems.

ORGANIZATIONAL PATTERNS

How well a family functions must be considered in terms of how well it organizes itself to meet the challenges life will send. Adaptability is one of the chief characteristics of family systems that work well. Flexibility, or the ability of a family to adapt to changing circumstances, is balanced by its need for stability, or enduring values; traditions; and predictable, consistent rules for behavior. Family adaptability can vary from very rigid to chaotic. Either extreme can cause problems.

Flexibility is required for a family to adapt to internal and external change. The family must be able to reorganize itself in response to the changes of life. Sometimes, a basic shift of rules is required. Crises, such as significant losses or changing social circumstances, stress the family and require major changes in family rules to ensure that family life goes on.

Dysfunctional families often resist making such changes because they rigidly adhere to rules about how their family is organized. For example, if a husband sustains an injury or illness that prevents him from working outside the home, he may need to assume homemaking responsibilities while his wife takes a job. A functional family will make this adjustment. A dysfunctional family with rigid role definitions, however, may refuse to change the major responsibilities of the husband and wife. The entire family may suffer economically and in other ways because of the family's lack of flexibility and its inability to adapt. Adhering to the rule that the husband earns the money and the wife takes care of the home is more important to this family than survival.

Other dysfunctional families break down because of the chaos in their organization. They lack any stability. Rules, for example, are constantly changing, and the children have no idea what is expected of them. Parents' standards are never the same.

BOUNDARY PROBLEMS

Chapter 3 mentioned problems with personal boundaries, which refers to the rules a family makes determining who does what, where, and when. Although family styles vary, dysfunctional families tend to have boundary problems characterized by extremes of either *disengagement* or *enmeshment*.

When parents pursue their interests or careers to the neglect of a child or adolescent, a pattern of disengagement can result, so that the young person feels little sense of connection to the family.

A disengaged pattern stresses individual differences, separateness, and distance at the expense of family unity. It goes to the extreme of fragmenting the family unit and isolating individual members. In some families, for instance, both parents pursue their own interests to the exclusion of caring for their children. Child care is left to employees or to older siblings. While the physical needs of the children may be met, the children do not receive nurturing from their parents and feel disconnected from them. The children may accomplish great things on the athletic field or in the classroom, but their parents' lack of interest in these achievements leaves the children feeling like they are not part of a connected family.

An enmeshed pattern, in contrast, limits or sacrifices individual differences to keep a sense of unity. Members are expected to think and feel alike: differences, privacy, and separation are seen as threats to the survival of the family. Typically, the child has little sense of self or has a distorted sense of self based on the parents' desires. Attempts by these children as adults to break loose from the family system are met with universal disapproval. The following case study, from the book *Toxic Parents*, by Susan Forward, is one example of boundary problems caused by an enmeshed pattern.

■   ■   ■

Fred is a young man whose mother had always made a big deal about everyone coming home for Christmas. When he was 26, Fred entered a radio contest and won a free trip to Aspen over the holidays. He decided he would take his girlfriend and looked forward to a great vacation. However, when he told these plans to his mother, she said with trembling lips, "It's okay, honey. You have a good time. Maybe we just won't have Christmas dinner this year."

Fred went on the trip anyway but had a miserable time. He spent half the time on the phone with his mother and siblings, apologizing for not being there. He later learned that his mother burned the Christmas turkey for the first time in 40 years.

"I got three phone calls from my sister telling me how I'd killed the family tradition," Fred reported. "My oldest brother told me everybody was totally bummed out because I wasn't there. And then my other brother really laid one on me. He said, 'Us kids are all she's got. How many more Christmases do you think Mom has left?' Like I'm abandoning her on her deathbed or something. Is that fair, Susan? She's not even sixty, she's in perfect health. I'm sure he got that line straight from my mother's mouth. I'll never miss Christmas again, I'll tell you that."

■   ■   ■

Because he had dared to do something different from the rest of the family, Fred was punished by everyone. And his initial response was exactly what they wanted to hear: he wouldn't miss Christmas again. Fred was falling back into line. As Fred's story shows, a functional family needs to be organized with boundaries that unite the family members but also allow for differences and individual independence.

Another type of organizational problem can occur when generational boundaries—the boundaries that define parent and child roles—begin to break down. Generational boundaries reinforce the essential leadership of the parents. Although it is common in single-parent or large families for elder children to assume parent-like caregiving responsibilities, such activity can become dysfunctional if rigid role expectations interfere with age-appropriate needs. A family in which a teen spends more time caring for a new baby brother than with school friends may verge on the dysfunctional.

A more destructive crossing of age boundaries occurs when a child becomes a surrogate spouse for a parent. In a family where the husband is addicted to work or is absent frequently for other reasons, the wife may turn to her oldest son for emotional intimacy. In reality, she should be seeking this support from her husband or from other adult friends. By expecting adult companionship from her son, she is crossing a necessary generational boundary and is committing emotional abuse. Her son becomes an emotional dumping ground, and because of the things his mother tells him about his father, his relationship with his father is also damaged. Crossing of the age boundary also occurs, obviously, when a parent commits physical sexual abuse.

Family-community boundaries are important as well. Functioning families are characterized by a clear sense of the family unit and flexible boundaries that connect the family to the community. Social networks extending through church, school, and other activities are important for the family. They provide support during difficult times and help the family develop a larger sense of community. When family members are isolated from the larger community, a dysfunctional situation is very likely to develop.

This single mother and her son are having a wonderful time together. In the future, though, if the mother depends too much on her son's companionship, generational boundaries could break down, creating a difficult emotional situation for both of them.

RELATIONSHIP TRIANGLES

Sometimes a triangle of relationships may develop. Three types of triangles typically occur. In the first kind of triangle, when tension develops between the husband and wife, they will try to draw in a third person. For instance, the couple may avoid their conflict by rallying together in concern for a child. Rather than focusing on their differences, the husband and wife may channel their energy toward a child's school or health problems.

In a second type of triangle, one family member teams with someone else in the family against a third person. Such triangles may be formed by a parent and child working together against the other parent, or by a grandparent-child team working against a single parent. The excluded family member supports this pattern by keeping his or her distance.

In a third arrangement, one family member may become a go-between for two others, balancing loyalties and regulating tension and intimacy. In divorced families or in marriages with serious problems, parents may use a child for this purpose.

In each case, all three members of the triangle are active participants, and each continues the pattern because together they are succeeding in reducing family tension. Unfortunately, in dysfunctional families these patterns do nothing to resolve underlying problems that need to be addressed. On the surface, peace is maintained, but as soon as something in life goes wrong, the underlying conflicts will explode.

COMMUNICATION AND PROBLEM SOLVING

Communication is vital for organizing and running a family. Every communication in a family has two functions: (1) communicating "content," such as facts, opinions, or feelings; and (2) communicating "relationship," the members' understanding of the nature of the family and their respective roles within it.

When a parent says, "Eat your vegetables," the message involves more than just vegetables. The parent also conveys an expectation that the child will obey and a sense that the parent is in charge. If the child spits out the vegetables, the child is indicating that the parent isn't in charge, at least not at this moment. Such relational communication cannot be left unclear or unresolved on a regular basis, or chaos will result. In a family evaluation, therefore, therapists assess the family members' abilities to communicate about both practical and emotional issues.

A father who is clearly angry but denies that anything is wrong leaves his children very confused. The content of his speech is at odds with the emotional messages he is conveying. A mother who chronically "forgets" to tell her family that she will be late getting home from work has a communication problem. Aside from the practical issues of life that are disrupted (should the others wait until Mom gets home before they eat dinner?), family members may interpret her forgetfulness as a message that they aren't important to her.

Along with communication difficulties, family therapists consider the family's problem-solving skills—that is, the family members' ability to resolve the problems they face and to keep the family functioning in effective ways. All families have problems, but functional families are

Family problems often involve communication difficulties. Frequently the trouble stems not from the "content" of a message but from its "relational" dimension—what it implies about the people's relationships.

able to solve them in a reasonable manner. When family function breaks down, families can struggle to resolve problems both with daily routines or responsibilities and with more difficult issues such as grief after divorce or death.

The problem-solving process has seven typical steps, and a family can falter at any of these:

1. Identifying the problem

2. Communicating with appropriate people about the problem

3. Developing a set of possible solutions

4. Deciding on one alternative

5. Carrying out the solution

6. Making sure the solution is carried out

7. Evaluating the effectiveness of the problem-solving process

LIFE-CYCLE DEVELOPMENT

A functional family sees itself as made up of many generations (at least three or four) moving forward over time. The individual's life takes place against the background of the family and its culture. The individual, family, and culture all change with the passing of time.

When treating a dysfunctional family, therapists find it very useful to note a connection between an individual's symptoms and both past and current critical events that have disrupted or threatened the family. To do this, they often take a family history.

A family history traces the family through several generations. This history includes family attitudes and beliefs, legacies and myths, taboos, rituals and traditions, loaded issues, fears, and expectations. It also describes the stresses a family faces. These include both predictable, everyday stresses and the unpredictable circumstances that can disrupt life, such as illness, a birth or death in the family, divorce, job loss, or natural disaster.

Families typically lack a perspective on time when a problem arises. Members can become overwhelmed by immediate feelings, feel stuck in the past (with an unresolved relationship, for instance), or be fixed on a future moment they dread (such as the death of a sick or injured loved one).

Relationships among family members evolve through stages as the family unit as a whole and all the individual members pass through the life cycle. Divorce and remarriage are additional life-cycle challenges for many families. Boundaries shift, and relationships are constantly being redefined. Each stage comes with its own set of issues and challenges.

Family symptoms and dysfunction often coincide with changes from one stage to another. All change (good or bad) is stressful, and it can be both good and bad at the same time. For example, the birth of a child, no matter how welcome, changes the balance of a family and may cause anxiety about money, loss of parental freedom, or intrusive grandparents, especially if one or both members of the couple remember similar reactions to the birth of a sibling in their own childhood. A positive

The boy at the right shows his jealousy as his grandparents admire his new sibling. The birth of a baby is frequently a critical point in the family life cycle.

experience as they go through this change can help the couple maintain their balance and perspective while they adjust to the new baby.

Many families function well until they reach the same critical point in the life cycle at which complications arose a generation earlier. For example, a father begins to have serious problems with his teenage son despite the good relationship they have had up to this point. When asked about his own teen years and his relationship with his father during that time, the man reveals that when he was 14 years old, his own father died. Without being able to draw upon the experience of relating to his father when he was a teenager, the man isn't sure how to relate to his own teenage son. Once the problem is identified, the therapist can help the man construct some ways to deal with his son.

BELIEF SYSTEMS

A family's response to stress is strongly influenced by its belief system. These beliefs contribute to the family's perception of events and to the ways in which it faces challenges.

Family members' beliefs about their ability to face and master life's challenges are particularly important. Fatalistic families believe that when bad things happen, there isn't much they can do. Such families are often overwhelmed by difficult situations because they don't try to deal with the problems. On the other hand, families that think normal life is problem-free have just as much difficulty dealing with problems because they don't expect problems to occur.

Family belief systems are derived from a number of sources. Important family stories provide guidelines for behavior when a family is facing a dilemma or crisis. These stories can either empower or weaken a family, depending both on the underlying themes of the stories and on whether they show the family adapting to circumstances in the past.

For instance, a family learned that the wife had irregular cells in her Pap smear. Rather than being encouraged by the doctor's assessment that this precancerous condition was highly treatable, the family members immediately became very depressed. The mother and grandmother of the wife had both died from ovarian cancer. Because of the often-repeated stories about the family's earlier fatal encounters with cancer, the family immediately assumed that the wife would get cancer and die. Family stories shaped their perceptions of and reactions to a challenging situation.

Family stories usually reflect the family's cultural, ethnic, and religious values. In one Armenian-American family, the parents and grandparents tell the children stories about the persecution the family endured in Armenia in the early 20th century. Many family members were imprisoned or killed by the Turks. Others fled to the United States. These stories communicate to the children the family's Orthodox Christian roots and the great value the elders place on political and religious freedom. They underscore the sacrifices the family has made to retain its Armenian identity and heritage.

A family that comes from two or more cultural or religious backgrounds must work hard to embrace all aspects of its heritage and to create a unique identity. Otherwise these differences can become a major source of conflict, particularly as young couples establish relationships with their extended families.

Family identity and beliefs are expressed through rituals. These rituals include holiday celebrations; weddings; funerals; religious services; and family traditions such as reunions, vacations, and birthday and anniversary celebrations. Rituals also include routine family interactions such as those at mealtimes and at bedtime. These rituals provide stability for the family when life is rough. Through them, family members can experience healing and be helped through transition periods in life, such as a death, suicide, miscarriage, or remarriage. This is why remembering birthdays, anniversaries, and other key dates in the family is so important for the family's well-being.

Once problem areas in a family's life have been identified, the opportunity for treatment and change begins. Dysfunctional families can learn how to function in healthy ways.

This young girl, born to a dysfunctional family and exposed in the womb to crack cocaine, had severe problems as an infant, but she thrived in the care of her foster mother, who later adopted her. The right therapy, combined with love, can do wonders.

5

MAJOR APPROACHES TO FAMILY THERAPY

To help members of dysfunctional families learn to relate to each other in new ways, several major approaches to family therapy have evolved. These can be grouped into the broad categories of problem-solving approaches and intergenerational approaches. Therapy sessions can be scheduled for one individual at a time or for combinations of family members.

Not all approaches are equally effective with all people. Often, only one or two members of the family are interested in changing their lives. In such cases, therapists help these family members make the changes in themselves that they desire and give them tools for responding in healthy ways to family members who are resistant to change.

PROBLEM-SOLVING APPROACHES

Problem-solving approaches focus on the particular problem that a family presents. Therapy tends to be relatively brief, and the goal is to design a practical intervention plan that will change the dysfunctional family pattern.

STRUCTURAL FAMILY THERAPY

One type of problem-solving approach, *structural family therapy*, emphasizes the importance of family organization in how the family unit functions. This method is based on the notion that imbalances in the family's organization cause problems, particularly if the boundaries between parents and children are unclear. The therapy centers on strengthening the family structure, with parents maintaining strong leadership and establishing clear boundaries that are neither too vague nor too rigid. The approach is action-oriented, focused on the problems rather than on the root causes. The assumption is that changes of behavior can occur even if the family members do not develop any deeper insight into the origin of their difficulties.

Structural family therapy is short-term and often involves three processes:

A father tries to settle an argument at dinner time. The need for strong, flexible leadership by the parents is one focus of structural family therapy.

joining, enactment, and restructuring. First, the therapist joins the family, assuming a position of leadership. Joining helps the therapist relate to and blend with the family to bring about change. Next, the therapist has the family enact its problem. In this process the therapist confronts and pushes the family members to test their flexibility and limits. Finally, the therapist employs tasks and guidelines that are designed to help the family restructure itself. The therapist gives special attention to strengthening the parents and reinforcing appropriate age boundaries.

The structural model is most often used when child-focused symptoms are present. Structural problems involving the extended family may also be addressed. For example, the therapist may confront boundary problems between a single-parent mother and a grandmother. Still, however, the focus of the treatment is not on exploring the origins of the conflict, but rather on restructuring the family arrangement so that symptoms are no longer reinforced by the family structure.

STRATEGIC/SYSTEMIC APPROACHES

Strategic/systemic approaches are another basic kind of problem-solving approach. They focus on the immediate social situation of the patient and its connection to the family system. Assuming that all problems have many causes, therapists view a problem as both a symptom and a response to current dysfunction in the way the family interacts.

In strategic/systemic approaches, it is important to understand how a family has already tried to resolve its problems, because a misguided solution may actually make the situation worse. Strategic therapists contend that most families do what they do because they believe it is the right or best way to approach a problem—or because it is the only way they know to try. The therapeutic task is to change the family's ways of handling the problem that do not work, while seeing the problem through the family members' eyes and taking into account their values and expectations.

Proponents of strategic/systemic approaches view "normal" families as being highly flexible, able to use a large assortment of behaviors to cope with problems. In contrast, a "pathological" family is rigid and sees few alternatives. Beyond this, each family must define what is normal or healthy for itself. The responsibility of the therapist is limited to initiating change that will free a family from unworkable solutions.

In therapies of this kind, the techniques of relabeling and reframing play a large role. Relabeling and reframing are ways of looking at a problem or a situation in a new light. Such redefinition can be particularly useful in changing a family's rigid view, in altering an unproductive blaming process ("It's always her fault"), and in overcoming resistance to change.

For example, a problem initially presented as being "inside" an individual, such as a character trait, can be redefined. A wife says she is depressed because her husband is unresponsive. He perceives her complaints about depression as an illegitimate attempt to get attention. In a

MAKING A PERSONAL CHANGE

Because children assume that their families are normal, children growing up in dysfunctional families usually don't realize until they are teens or adults that their families have serious problems.

If you think you were or are part of a dysfunctional family, the Counseling Center at the University of Illinois, Urbana-Champaign, suggests that it may be helpful to consider the following actions as you begin to rethink and reorganize your life:

- Although it may be disturbing, identify painful or difficult experiences from your childhood. Often a first step in beginning to change is facing up to the difficulties that you've experienced.

- Make a list of your behaviors, beliefs, and other things you would like to change. Beside each item, write how you would like to act or think instead. Pick one item on your list and begin practicing the alternative behavior or belief. Choose the easiest item first, and once you are able to act or think in the new way more often than in the original way, pick another item on the list and practice changing it, too.

- You may find it helpful to work with a professional counselor or with a group of people who had similar experiences during childhood.

- Don't attempt to be perfect or to make your family perfect.

- Set clear limits. Say no, not maybe.

- Recognize that when you stop behaving or thinking in the way you used to, there may be negative reactions from your family or friends. Anticipate these reactions and decide how you will respond.

Source: Adapted from University of Illinois at Urbana-Champaign Counseling Center, "Understanding Dysfunctional Relationship Patterns in Your Family." Available at http://www.odos.uiuc.edu/Counseling_Center/dysfunct.htm.

vicious circle, the more she complains, the more he withdraws, and the more he withdraws, the more upset she becomes. Changing the way her problem is described or labeled and determining a variety of causes for her depression may break this unhealthy process.

Directives may also be useful. Directives are tasks that therapists

The first step in changing a dysfunctional family is for the family members to face up to their problems.

assign to families to be carried out either in a session or between sessions—a kind of family "homework." Directives have several purposes. They are used to gather information about the ways family members interact and how they will respond to change and begin to encourage change.

Many strategic/systemic therapists see the symptom as essentially an act of communication, part of a repetitive sequence that occurs among the family members. If they break the "feedback" loop that supports the symptom, they can help the family alter the dysfunctional pattern.

BEHAVIORAL APPROACHES

Behavioral approaches to family therapy emphasize the importance of family rules and communication, as well as a practical approach to solving the particular problem that has arisen. Behavioral approaches focus on the interaction between family members and the conditions under which their behavior is learned, influenced, and changed. These approaches have been especially helpful in resolving marital conflicts and helping families of children and adolescents who are behaving in inappropriate ways.

The goal of behavioral therapy in family relationships is to have the family stop reinforcing inappropriate behavior. Instead, the family learns how to reward positive change through attention, acknowledgment, and approval. For instance, a child who feels neglected may frequently disrupt family meals to get attention. Instead of reinforcing that behavior with the attention the child craves, the parents learn to use attention and approval to reward more positive behavior.

Relationships may also become strained by communication problems that result when there is a difference between an intended message and the way the receiver interprets it. Behavioral therapists try to pinpoint such difficulties and help family members overcome them. Negotiation and problem-solving skills are stressed, as is flexibility.

INTERGENERATIONAL APPROACHES

In contrast to problem-solving approaches, which tend to focus on very specific, short-term goals, *intergenerational approaches* to family therapy are more exploratory and oriented toward the family's long-term growth. They pay attention to the systemic processes that occur during the ongoing development of the family and of its individual members. These approaches are called "intergenerational" because they emphasize not only the relationships of parents with children, but also the continuing effects of patterns that existed in earlier generations. In particular, intergenerational approaches pay a great deal of attention to the parents' families of origin—that is, the families in which the parents themselves grew up.

The parents are seen as the keys to family functioning. Did the parents have negative or disturbing childhood experiences that are impairing their interactions with their children? Do they have unresolved conflicts or past losses that interfere with their responses to other family members? Symptoms of such a conflict or loss may disrupt the entire pattern of the family's interaction. If so, the therapist helps the family understand the origin of the problem and identify the ways it is affecting the family system. Then, with the therapist's guidance and encouragement, family members work with each other to confront the difficulties and find solutions.

In some variants of this approach, the therapist constructs a time line to discover patterns in the occurrence of symptoms and critical family events. Sometimes a patient may be asked to contact members of the extended family in order to fill in missing information.

Since the approach is long-term, family members focus first on

This young mother, considered a "high-risk" parent because she herself came from an abusive family, volunteered for a study on the cycle of child abuse. Her willingness to work on the problem was a big step toward breaking the cycle.

gaining a better perspective on the problems that are occurring and the reasons for them. The therapist may encourage each family member to see the situation from the others' points of view, putting aside emotional reactions in order to seek intellectual clarity. The goal is for each family member to gain a fuller awareness of himself or herself in relation to the others in the family. Only when this understanding has developed does the therapy turn toward identifying and promoting a new, more positive set of behaviors.

MODES OF FAMILY THERAPY

Whatever approach is used, the therapist may schedule sessions with one or more family members, the husband and wife as a pair, the entire family as a group, or an even larger number of people such as a multi-family group. Each mode of therapy has particular uses.

FAMILY GROUP THERAPY

In *family group therapy*, the therapist works with the entire family as a group. This is particularly useful for a family with a child- or adolescent-focused problem. Parents, siblings, and any other significant members of the household or extended family are treated together.

Family group therapy is useful for a range of other problems as well. Separation, divorce, and remarriage involve a number of family issues that are often best addressed by joint sessions. Other situations in which family group therapy may be helpful include chronic psychiatric and medical conditions; major stressful life events such as work difficulties or loss through death; and situations involving substance, sexual, or physical abuse. If a problem is identified as being strongly connected to unresolved issues within the family, it is typically best treated with the entire family.

In the early days of family group therapy, some people believed it was inevitably more superficial than one-on-one treatment. Now this view is generally held to be a myth. In one-on-one therapy, the therapist is frequently trying to treat symptoms of a problem that involves others. By bringing other family members into the therapeutic sessions, the therapist gains an opportunity to address the larger picture and perhaps acquires more power to alter situations that cause the issue.

For many problems, as John Rolland and Froma Walsh point out in a review of family therapy, an exclusive individual therapy may achieve certain individual goals of growth, but that growth may come at the cost of a marriage or family unit. Often individuals with relationship difficulties or problems with intimacy are in a troubled relationship at the time of treatment. Deciding to work with the individual without seeing his or her spouse as well, for example, can leave the therapist with a one-sided view of the problem. The patient may "grow," but the family or couple relationship may not survive. The caring, empathic therapeutic relationship may also make other real-life relationships seem even less satisfactory by comparison. In fact, research cited by Rolland and Walsh suggests that individual therapy in distressed marriages skews the couple toward divorce. Also, a troubled relationship may not be able to remain on hold for as long as it would take for the individual spouse to complete therapeutic treatment.

Short-term treatment of families and couples (called *brief treatment*) has been particularly useful when the chief complaint is a particular behavior, situation, or regular life-cycle transition. Early marriage, parenthood, children leaving home, caring for aging parents, and retirement are times when couples or families are confronted with new challenges that bring to the surface preexisting family strains or conflicts. An early-intervention approach with a family can avert a major crisis.

When a specific or focal problem is being addressed, the therapist and family frequently contract for a certain number of sessions. The goals for the sessions are clearly outlined, and progress can be monitored. This approach is similar to individual brief treatment. At the completion of the contract, the therapist and family can renegotiate a new brief contract or sometimes shift to a more open-ended exploration of a family's relationships.

Some families learn to use family consultations and treatment occasionally as family strains emerge during the life cycle. Some family therapists find this kind of arrangement well suited to certain families and situations. This approach is particularly useful for families coping with chronic psychiatric or physical disorders in which new life-cycle challenges keep emerging as the continuing condition changes.

COUPLES THERAPY

A problem identified by a family as a "couple's" problem would likely be treated as such, excluding children just as one would close the bedroom door. When patients have problems of intimacy and are currently in a primary relationship with a partner or spouse, therapy for the couple is generally indicated.

Couples therapy is the treatment of choice for serious relationship conflict and communication problems. Destructive interaction patterns that can escalate into violence or lead to the end of the relationship can be changed through early treatment. Couples therapy is also useful when a couple is undergoing a major change in their roles—for

When a husband and wife have serious communication difficulties, couples therapy may be the best treatment method.

instance, when one partner is affected by a serious illness and the other partner will likely need to provide ongoing support or care.

INDIVIDUAL SYSTEMIC THERAPY

Individual systemic therapy focuses primarily on sessions with the individual patient, but also explores the family as a system. A particular version of this, termed "family coaching," is growing in popularity.

In family coaching, the therapeutic goal is to change the patient's relationships with his or her family of origin. In the individual sessions, the therapist helps the patient connect current problems with unresolved relationship issues. Then, often, the sessions are extended to include other key family members, and the therapist helps the patient work toward resolving the relationship problems. For instance, if a father's problems with his teenager stem from the man's unresolved feelings toward his own father, one or more sessions might bring the father and grandfather together.

MULTIFAMILY GROUP THERAPY

Multifamily group therapy was first developed for young adults hospitalized with psychotic disorders. In recent years, multifamily group approaches have expanded to address a wider range of psychiatric conditions. In particular, such interventions have been utilized for the treatment of depression.

Groups are typically composed of four or more patients with their families, including parents, siblings, spouses, and sometimes close friends. The objectives of the group typically include improving communication and structural patterns in the family so that the amount of stress is reduced and the family improves its overall functioning and problem solving. Some such groups meet for a short term only, ranging from a single, day-long workshop to a specified and limited number of sessions. Other groups are open-ended and ongoing.

The group provides support while family members try out new ways of relating. It also offers opportunities for each family to learn from other families. Family members can relate to the experience of their counterparts in other families, gain a perspective on their own situation, reduce guilt and blame, and feel less isolated.

Ongoing multifamily or couples therapy groups are useful alternatives to other forms of treatment. This is particularly true for situations in which ongoing stress is inevitable, as when a family is living with a chronic disorder such as Alzheimer's disease. Often these families feel isolated because their friends have never experienced a similar situation and don't understand the daily stresses the family undergoes. When friends try to help, they often offer inappropriate suggestions because they don't understand the dynamics of the situation.

Multifamily or couples therapy groups allow such isolated families to establish support networks with families facing similar kinds of problems. These networks often extend well beyond the group sessions. Knowing that another family is experiencing the same kinds of struggles can be very reassuring to a family in crisis. Also, the families in the group make each other aware of resources and tools that are uniquely helpful to new situations a family confronts.

COMBINED THERAPIES

It is more and more common for families to use *combined therapies*—both multiple therapists and multiple therapy approaches. This is certainly true for families living with chronic psychiatric disorders such as schizophrenia or with serious physical conditions such as Lou Gehrig's disease. At any one time an individual may be involved in individual, couples, family, and multifamily group treatments to address various aspects of the situation that faces the family.

Often, couples or family therapy begins after one or more members of the family is already in individual treatment. The challenge for the therapist is to make the treatment system work effectively. For example, when one partner is already in individual treatment, a couples therapist may find it appropriate for the other partner to begin individual treatment so that both members of the couple are addressing individual issues as well as working together on problems in their relationship.

Some people question whether it is advisable for a family therapist to conduct individual therapy with a family member as well as with the family as a whole. The same question is raised about individual therapists who conduct sessions with a patient's family. However, many family therapists make a point of including individual sessions in their therapeutic approach. They argue that meeting with individual members of the family allows them to get a more complete picture of the family situation.

This is particularly true when communication is guarded or very volatile. If a family has an unwritten rule not to share secrets of physical, emotional, or substance abuse with outsiders, the therapist is much more likely to learn of such behavior through conversations with individual members of the family. Similarly, if one family member dominates everyone else in the family, other members may be afraid of expressing themselves freely as long as that person is present.

Sometimes in the course of treatment, a family member is obviously reluctant to speak openly with other family members. A child may be afraid to speak to a domineering parent, or a spouse may avoid confronting an overbearing partner. In such cases, individual sessions can help these people deal with the issues that cause their fear and help them overcome their reluctance to talk with the other family members. Then treatment of the family group can move ahead.

Likewise, therapists may include joint sessions in the course of individual therapy to help their client work through issues with a specific family member. Careful planning, timing, and focus are important in such sessions, and the therapist must prepare so that neither the patient nor the other family member will be able to take over the session. For instance, if a woman wants to confront her father about abuse that took place during her childhood, the therapist may arrange to hold a meeting

Using the method of combined therapies, this family therapist (right) works with the family as a whole and also with individual family members.

between the two family members. Part of the therapist's role during the meeting would be to prevent the father from verbally attacking his daughter, treating her with disrespect, or trying to change the subject of the discussion.

In some situations it is clearly advantageous to have one therapist conduct both the individual and family treatments. An example would be an inpatient or partial hospitalization program with a built-in time limit for treatment. In such a situation, the patient's therapist is in the best position to carry out family treatments that are meant to educate or support the family to which the hospitalized patient will be returning. The therapist's understanding of the patient informs his or her work with the larger family group.

A family consultation may also enhance other treatment plans. For example, in arranging drug therapy, a therapist can discuss the treatment plan with the patient and family together. This approach encourages family support and helps reduce resistance to treatment once the patient returns to his or her home.

Roy Campanella talks with his children in 1959, a year after his great baseball career was ended by an auto accident that left him permanently disabled. Long-term illnesses and disabilities create special challenges for any family.

6

SPECIAL SITUATIONS

Certain psychiatric and physical disorders create unique challenges for family therapy. While the general principles of family therapy are applicable to these situations, therapists can better help the family when they keep specific issues in mind during treatment.

SERIOUS MENTAL DISORDERS

Over the past several decades, research on major mental disorders has revealed a complicated relationship between biological and social factors. The clinical theory and research on the role of the family in schizophrenia provide a good example.

In the 1940s and 1950s it was assumed that faulty mothering in early childhood caused schizophrenia. Then, beginning in the late 1950s, a new view of the family led to the idea that the family played a role in the development of the disorder, especially if the family had disordered structure, poor communication, and relational problems. With few exceptions, these early studies were flawed and lacked independent confirmation. Nevertheless, theories that the family caused schizophrenia were popular and understandably tended to traumatize those families whose members were affected by the disorder.

More recent family studies, which assume that both biological and environmental factors have an ongoing influence on patients, have shifted focus from the development of the disorder to attempts to understand its future course and outcome. The most promising line of inquiry has examined family attitudes and ways of communicating.

In the 1970s, researchers found evidence linking schizophrenia with certain attitudes expressed by family members, presumably reflecting ongoing family interactions. The concept of "expressed emotion" was developed to explain the finding that critical comments and emotional overinvolvement often occurred before a patient relapsed into schizophrenic behavior. In particular, the research revealed an association between relapse and highly expressed emotion by spouses and other relatives. These findings suggested that family relationships are crucial both in the course of the illness and in intervention.

Researchers began to pay attention to the importance of strengthening and supporting the families of patients with serious mental disorders. Investigators realized that the dysfunctional family patterns seen when a patient is in crisis may not reflect the family's best level of functioning. Instead, the family's unhealthy behaviors may be the result of the stress of the crisis. While families influence individual members, those individual members by their disturbed behavior in turn affect the family.

In the early 1970s, patients who had been living in mental hospitals and other institutions began to be placed in the community for a variety of reasons, including changes in state and federal programs and funding. This deinstitutionalization movement failed to include adequate outpatient services for the released patients. Changes in institutional and governmental policies further reduced the number and length of hospital stays. While regular use of prescription medications could help control psychotic symptoms of patients, by itself these medications were not enough to enable them to function independently in the community.

As the families of these released patients faced society's expectation that they would assume the primary caregiving role for their mentally ill family members, they quickly realized that they needed more support from the larger community. Many of them organized through the National Alliance for the Mentally Ill (NAMI) and other groups to campaign for more supportive programs and community resources.

The availability of community programs that offer support to families dealing with a serious mental disorder has a great impact on how both the patient and the larger family adapt to their situation. So does the acceptance or stigma associated with mental illness in the community.

In designing clinical treatment for patients and families, family intervention priorities should include the following:

- Information about the illness, the need for treatments, patient abilities and limitations, and the prognosis

- Concrete guidelines for stress reduction and problem solving through different phases of the illness

A man diagnosed with schizophrenia tries a mountain bike. His friend belongs to a volunteer group dedicated to befriending people afflicted with psychiatric disorders. Such community support groups are vital in the adaptation of both patients and their families.

- Available services that support the efforts of families to maintain the patient in the community

Educational approaches, in which the patient and the family are fully informed about the illness and treatment, have best demonstrated their usefulness with illnesses like schizophrenia. According to studies surveyed by John Rolland and Froma Walsh, educational approaches delay relapse, reduce family stress, improve functioning for both schizophrenic patients and their families, and show promise in treating severe affective disorders.

It is important to recognize the need for combined intervention strategies in the treatment of serious and chronic psychiatric disorders. For instance, the combination of family therapy with drug therapy has been found to be more effective than either one alone in preventing relapse in schizophrenia. Adding patient involvement in a social skills group to those treatments yields the best results.

Brief problem-solving family therapy may be of use to many families with a range of serious disorders. By focusing on clear, concrete, and realistic objectives that can be reached through weekly sessions over several months, families have experienced improved functioning and reduced stress and conflict. By attending monthly or periodic maintenance sessions, multiple family therapy groups, or self-help organizations, families have more success sustaining their gains and averting serious setbacks.

Crisis intervention should be available to families in times of acute distress, because most chronic, severe disorders involve periods when symptoms get worse. Therapists must be active and provide enough structure to help temporarily disorganized and overwhelmed families gain perspective and control of threatening situations.

Because patients with serious disorders, especially schizophrenia, may lack motivation to attend treatment or may fail to take their medication, family support is crucial. Such intervention helps keep patients in treatment and helps family members cope with acute episodes in ways that will keep stress at manageable levels. Without such guidance, many families go from one crisis to the next, achieve few gains over time, and risk emotional exhaustion. Eventually, they may simply give up on the patient and cut him or her off from the family.

For these reasons, therapists find it helpful for everyone involved if they contract with the family to use relatively calm times for anticipating and preventing future crises. During these periods family members have more energy to deal with such issues than they do in the middle of a crisis.

While complete cures have not been developed for many serious psychiatric disorders, the conditions can usually be made more manageable. Although it may take time to find the right combination and dosage of medications for a given individual, prescription drugs can moderate the symptoms of biologically based illnesses. In effective treatment, the family is viewed as an indispensable ally. Together, therapists and family members can work to reduce family stress, strengthen the ability of the family to function in a supportive way, and improve the patient's ability to function.

CHRONIC PHYSICAL CONDITIONS

Most families face health crises or serious illness in a family member at some point. Any health crisis or chronic (long-lasting) illness or disability has a profound impact on the entire family. Complex interactions involving the illness, patient, medical professionals, and family members extend over the course of any chronic condition.

For a decade or more, some health professionals have been developing a family-systems approach to chronic physical conditions. In studying the relationship of illness to family life cycles, these professionals often divide the family's response to an illness or disability into at least two distinct phases.

The *crisis* phase is the initial period of adjusting to chronic illness. Parents learn that their teenage daughter has been paralyzed in a car accident. A mother who has been experiencing difficulty keeping her

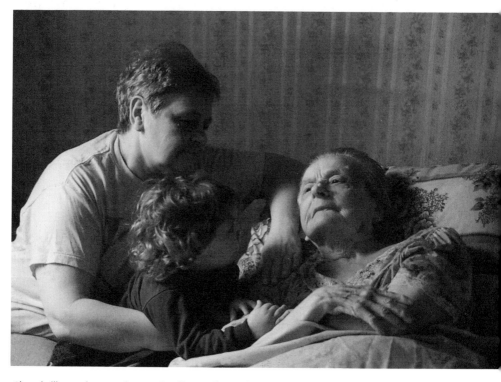

Chronic illness changes the way family members relate to one another. If the family struggles to adjust, therapy can help.

A boy with Down syndrome celebrates his birthday with his family. Children with Down syndrome, a chromosome disorder that results in mental retardation, are especially dependent on their families for love and support.

balance is diagnosed with multiple sclerosis. A father develops heart disease and is placed on permanent disability, requiring that he stop work at the age of 40. As family members absorb these shocking pieces of news, they attempt to do six things:

1. Create meaning for the disorder (why did this happen?)
2. Mourn the loss of the pre-illness family identity
3. Accept, when necessary, the permanency of the condition
4. Undergo short-term crisis reorganization while developing family flexibility in the face of uncertainty and possible loss
5. Learn to live with illness-related symptoms and treatments
6. Set up a working relationship with professionals and institutions, as needed

Once the initial adjustment to the situation is over, the reality of its permanence settles in. Family members begin to accept that the changes brought by the illness are going to be with them for a long time. In this *chronic* phase, families deal with four issues:

1. Pacing their emotions to avoid burnout. Like a marathon runner, family members in chronic situations cannot sprint through the course of life. Once the crisis phase ends, they must learn to expend their energy deliberately so that they will be able to live long-term with the situation.
2. Negotiating changes in relationships between the patient and other family members. Chronic illness changes family roles, and this by definition creates changes in how people relate to each other.
3. Preserving the goals of the family and of each member within the constraints of the illness. While the financial and physical limitations of an illness need to be accepted, the illness shouldn't define the family and its members.
4. Sustaining intimacy in the face of threatened loss. The possible loss of lifestyle or life causes some family members to withdraw from each other. But while relationships are changing, the family's underlying closeness can be preserved.

A therapist's assessment of a family facing chronic physical illness or disability may include observations about a wide range of family dynamics:

- The family's health/illness belief system

- The family's multigenerational history of coping with illness, loss, and crisis

- Illness-oriented communication, problem solving, and role flexibility

- Social support and use of community resources

- The family's ability to manage illness-related crises or perform home-based medical care

Ideally, the therapist takes many such matters into account in designing an appropriate program of counseling and treatment. Support groups made up of families dealing with similar physical disorders can also help families tap into community resources.

SUBSTANCE ABUSE

For many years, substance-abuse treatment programs, particularly those designed for alcoholism, have included a family component. However, many of these programs have historically treated the family separately from the addicted member. This is the practice followed by 12-step self-help programs such as Alcoholics Anonymous and Al-Anon as well as by numerous drug treatment approaches. Many people have been greatly helped through these programs, but their separation of family counseling from individual treatment may mean that the family system as a whole is not fully addressed.

Recently, innovative models based on family-systems concepts have also been used to treat alcoholism and drug abuse. Central to these approaches is an awareness that chronic substance abuse becomes a central fact in families' lives, which means that any long-term solution needs family cooperation and involvement in treatment.

Family involvement in the development of a comprehensive treatment plan has been successful in reducing the high rate of treatment failure caused by dropout from detoxification and early relapse. A family history can help identify substance abuse in other family members and other behaviors that might threaten successful treatment.

The current trend in substance-abuse treatment focuses less on residential rehabilitation and more on outpatient therapy, such as partial hospitalization or evening programs. Because these programs keep the patient at home, family-based treatment becomes even more important.

FAMILY CHALLENGES: DIVORCE AND REMARRIAGE

As the divorce rate rises, single-parent households and stepfamilies have become increasingly common. Of those people who divorce, 75 percent of men and 65 percent of women eventually remarry. Current estimates indicate that blended families resulting from divorce and remarriage are becoming the most common form of American family.

Research finds a wide range of adaptation to divorce and remarriage among families. Some parents and children do poorly, but most fare reasonably well over time (and as many as a third function at a high level). When children fare poorly, their problems are not related to the divorce per se, but to serious preexisting problems in the family combined with the failure of their parents to manage the divorce process without adding to the conflict. When contact and/or financial support from the noncustodial parent is broken off, children also suffer. More than half of noncustodial fathers fail to provide reliable support for and regular contact with their children.

Children are also burdened when they are caught up in parental battles or shuttled back and forth between households under a joint-custody arrangement that splits the children's time and emotional energies. Child adjustment is best when there is a solid home base, when biological parents cooperate in parenting without creating ongoing conflict, and when the noncustodial parent maintains reliable contact, care, and support.

Clinical intervention and divorce mediation are highly recommended to help parents work through losses, buffer the stresses and dislocation, plan workable financial and custody arrangements, reorganize to manage the demands of heading a single-parent household, and forge a collaborative coparental arrangement. Some states require divorced parents of dependent children to go through such treatment.

Therapeutic efforts are usefully directed toward helping families

The long-running sitcom The Brady Bunch *presented an ideal version of a large blended family created by the parents' remarriage. In real life, however, the children of divorced or remarried parents face many challenges.*

accomplish these tasks in the divorce process and establish a workable and flexible family structure after the divorce. When one or the other parent later remarries, therapists can help sort out the complex network of new relationships, solidify the new family unit, and encourage flexible boundaries to allow children to maintain their relationships with both biological parents and extended families as they develop new steprelations.

Although the situations described in this chapter put families under increasing stress, it is important to realize that such pressures do not force families into dysfunctional patterns. With the help of a wide range of treatment options, both the family and its individual members can learn to work together to build a family unit that is truly supportive and functional for the good of all.

APPENDIX

FOR MORE INFORMATION

The following are good sources for general information on dysfunctional families and on coping with the psychological conditions that living with a dysfunctional family may create. In addition, family support programs and information hotlines are listed in the telephone directories of almost every city. Many hospitals and medical centers sponsor family programs and provide information as well. Schools, colleges, and religious organizations are also good sources for information.

American Academy of Child and Adolescent Psychiatry (AACAP)
3615 Wisconsin Ave., NW
Washington, DC 20016-3007
(202) 966-7300
http://www.aacap.org/

C. Henry Kempe National Center for Prevention and Treatment of Child Abuse and Neglect
1205 Oneida St.
Denver, CO 80220
(303) 321-3963

The Dougy Center, The National Center for Grieving Children and Families
P.O. Box 86852
Portland, OR 97286
(503) 775-5683
fax: (503) 777-3097
http://www.dougy.org/

National Alliance for the Mentally Ill Child and Adolescent Network (NAMI-CAN)
200 North Glebe Rd.
Suite 1015
Arlington, VA 22203-3754
(800) 950-NAMI

National Coalition Against Domestic Violence
P.O. Box 34103
Washington, DC 20043-4103
(202) 638-6388
TTY (202) 737-3033

National Committee to Prevent Child Abuse (NCPCA)
332 South Michigan Ave.
Suite 1600
Chicago, IL 60604
(800) CHILDREN, (312) 663-3520
publications: (800) 55-NCPCA

National Council on Child Abuse and Family Violence
1155 Connecticut Ave., NW
Suite 400
Washington, DC 20036
(800) 222-2000, (202) 429-6695

National Domestic Violence Hotline
1-800-799-SAFE (7233)
http://www.nduh.org/

National Information Center for Children and Youth with Disabilities (NICHCY)
P.O. Box 1492
Washington, DC 20013
(800) 695-0285
http://www.nichcy.org/

National Institute of Child Health and Human Development (NICHD)
NICHD Clearinghouse
P.O. Box 30006
Rockville, MD 20847
(800) 370-2943
fax: (301) 984-1473
e-mail: NICHDClearinghouse
@iqsolutions.com

National Institute of Mental Health (NIMH)
NIMH Public Inquiries
6001 Executive Boulevard
Room 8184 MSC 9663
Bethesda, MD 20892-9663
e-mail: nimhinfo@nih.gov
http://www.nimh.nih.gov/

National Network for Youth
1319 F St., NW
Suite 401
Washington, DC 20004
(202) 783-7949

APPENDIX

BIBLIOGRAPHY

American Psychiatric Association. *Diagnostic and Statistical Manual of Mental Disorders.* 4th ed. Washington, D.C.: American Psychiatric Press, 1994.

Annie E. Casey Foundation. *1998 Kids Count Online.* Available at http://www.aecf.org/kidscount/.

Forward, Susan. *Toxic Parents.* New York: Bantam Books, 1989.

Halpern, Howard M. *Cutting Loose.* New York: Fireside, 1990.

Kadis, Leslie B., and Ruth McClendon, "Family Therapy: Systems Approaches to Assessment and Treatment." In Robert E. Hales, Stuart C. Yudofsky, and John A. Talbott, *The American Psychiatric Press Textbook of Psychiatry*, 3d ed. Washington, D.C.: American Psychiatric Press, 1999.

Mellody, Pia, Andrea Wells Miller, and J. Keith Miller. *Facing Codependence: What It Is; Where It Comes From; How It Sabotages Our Lives.* San Francisco: HarperSanFrancisco, 1989.

"Mick's TV Teen Conquest." *Wall of Sound*, March 5, 1999. Available at http://wallofsound.go.com/news/stories/jagger030599.html.

Osterkamp, Lynn. *How to Deal with Your Parents When They Still Treat You Like a Child.* New York: Berkley Books, 1992.

Pipher, Mary. *Reviving Ophelia: Saving the Selves of Adolescent Girls.* New York: Ballantine Books, 1994.

Pro, Johnna A. "Welfare Mom's Fatal Choice." *Pittsburgh Post-Gazette*, March 18, 1999.

Rolland, John S., and Froma Walsh. "Family Therapy: Systems Approaches to Assessment and Treatment." In Robert E. Hales, Stuart C. Yudofsky, and John A. Talbott, *The American Psychiatric Press Textbook of Psychiatry*, 2d ed. Washington, D.C.: American Psychiatric Press, 1994.

U.S. Bureau of the Census. "Census Bureau Facts for Features." CB99-FF.03. February 23, 1999. Available at http://www.census.gov/.

U.S. Bureau of the Census. *Population Profile of the United States: 1997.* Current Population Reports, Series P23-194. Washington, D.C.: U.S. Government Printing Office, 1998.

University of Illinois at Urbana-Champaign Counseling Center. "Understanding Dysfunctional Relationship Patterns in Your Family." Available at http://www.odos.uiuc.edu/Counseling_Center/dysfunct.htm.

Ventura, Stephanie, Joyce Martin, Sally Curtin, and T. J. Mathews. *Report of Final Natality Statistics, 1996.* PHS 98-1120. Washington, D.C.: U.S. Department of Health and Human Services.

Wallace, Barbara C. *Adult Children of Dysfunctional Families: Prevention, Intervention, and Treatment for Community Mental Health Promotion.* Westport, Conn.: Praeger Publishers, 1996.

APPENDIX

FURTHER READING

Coman, Carolyn. *What Jamie Saw*. New York: Puffin, 1997.

De Vries, Anke. *Bruises*. Trans. Stacey Knecht. Asheville, N.C.: Front Street Press, 1996.

Forward, Susan. *Toxic Parents*. New York: Bantam Books, 1989.

Franklin, Kristine L. *Eclipse*. Cambridge, Mass.: Candlewick Press, 1998.

Fraustino, Lisa Rowe. *Ash: A Novel*. New York: Orchard Books, 1995.

Grant, Cynthia D. *Shadow Man*. New York: Atheneum, 1992.

Lowery, Linda. *Laurie Tells*. Minneapolis: Carolrhoda Books, 1994.

McDonald, Megan. *The Bridge to Nowhere*. New York: Orchard Books, 1993.

Mellody, Pia, Andrea Wells Miller, and J. Keith Miller. *Facing Codependence: What It Is; Where It Comes From; How It Sabotages Our Lives*. San Francisco: HarperSanFrancisco, 1989.

Morris, Winifred. *Liar*. New York: Walker & Co., 1996.

Voigt, Cynthia. *When She Hollers*. New York: Scholastic, 1994.

Wartski, Maureen. *Dark Silence*. New York: Juniper, 1994.

Weinstein, Nina J. *No More Secrets*. Seattle: Seal Press, 1991.

Behavioral approaches: approaches to family therapy that aim to have the family stop reinforcing inappropriate behavior. They emphasize the importance of family rules and communication, as well as a practical approach to solving problems.

Blended family: a family that consists of stepparents and stepchildren.

Combined therapies: the use of multiple therapists and/or multiple approaches to therapy. At any one time an individual may be involved in individual, group, family, and multifamily group treatments to address various aspects of the situation that faces the family.

Complex family: a family that is based either on generational ties (including grandparents or great-grandparents) or lateral ties (including aunts, uncles, and cousins).

Consanguineal family: a family made up of a single parent and his or her children.

Couples therapy: therapy in which the two members of a couple meet together with a therapist. Children and other family members are not included in the sessions.

Directives: tasks assigned to a family by a therapist. These assignments are to be carried out either in a session or between sessions, a kind of family "homework."

Disengagement: a family pattern that emphasizes individual differences, separateness, and distance at the expense of family unity. When taken to an extreme, this pattern fragments the family unit and isolates individual members.

Dysfunctional family: a family that fails to provide for its members' physical and/or emotional needs. Children are often expected to carry adult responsibilities while one or both parents behave in childishly irresponsible ways.

Enmeshment: a family pattern that limits or sacrifices individual differences to keep a sense of overall unity. Family members are expected to think and feel alike. Differences, privacy, and separation are seen as threats to the survival of the family.

Family group therapy: an approach to therapy in which the therapist works with the entire family as a group. This is particularly helpful for families with a child- or adolescent-focused problem. Parents, siblings, and any other significant members of the household or extended family are treated together.

Individual systemic therapy: a cross between systemic treatment and individual treatment. The therapist uses both individual sessions and sessions that include other key family members to resolve problems.

Intergenerational approaches: approaches to family therapy that are oriented to a family's long-term growth. They tend to be more time-consuming and exploratory than problem-solving approaches, and they typically emphasize the effects of earlier generations of the family on later ones.

Multifamily group therapy: a type of therapy in which several patients and their families meet together with a therapist to improve communication and patterns within each family, reduce stress, improve the way each family functions, and solve problems.

Nuclear family: a husband, a wife, and their children living together in an independent or separate household.

Problem-solving approaches: approaches to family therapy that focus on a specific problem and aim for a practical solution that can be achieved in a relatively short time.

Strategic/systemic approaches: systems-oriented, problem-solving approaches to therapy that focus on the immediate situation of the patient. A problem is viewed as both a symptom and a response to current dysfunction in the way the family interacts.

Structural family therapy: an approach to family therapy that centers on strengthening the family structure, with parents maintaining strong leadership and establishing clear boundaries that are neither too vague nor too rigid. Therapy is designed to change dysfunctional organizational patterns so that the family can better perform basic tasks and cope with stress.

APPENDIX

INDEX

APPENDIX

PICTURE CREDITS

Senior Consulting Editor Carol C. Nadelson, M.D., is president and chief executive officer of the American Psychiatric Press, Inc., staff physician at Cambridge Hospital, and Clinical Professor of Psychiatry at Harvard Medical School. In addition to her work with the American Psychiatric Association, which she served as vice president in 1981–83 and president in 1985–86, Dr. Nadelson has been actively involved in other major psychiatric organizations, including the Group for the Advancement of Psychiatry, the American College of Psychiatrists, the Association for Academic Psychiatry, the American Association of Directors of Psychiatric Residency Training Programs, the American Psychosomatic Society, and the American College of Mental Health Administrators. In addition, she has been a consultant to the Psychiatric Education Branch of the National Institute of Mental Health and has served on the editorial boards of several journals. Doctor Nadelson has received many awards, including the Gold Medal Award for significant and ongoing contributions in the field of psychiatry, the Elizabeth Blackwell Award for contributions to the causes of women in medicine, and the Distinguished Service Award from the American College of Psychiatrists for outstanding achievements and leadership in the field of psychiatry.

Consulting Editor Claire E. Reinburg, M.A., is editorial director of the American Psychiatric Press, Inc., which publishes about 60 new books and six journals a year. She is a graduate of Georgetown University in Washington, D.C., where she earned bachelor of arts and master of arts degrees in English. She is a member of the Council of Biology Editors, the Women's National Book Association, the Society for Scholarly Publishing, and Washington Book Publishers.

Ann Holmes has written and edited professionally for over 16 years. Her special areas of interest are cultural and medical topics. She is also the editor of *The Loyalhanna Review*, the annual literary journal of the Ligonier Valley Writers. She and her family live in southwestern Pennsylvania.